For Tony & Michele —
with warm regards.

John Manesis
November 5, 2009

WITH ALL MY BREATH

Library of Congress Card Catalog Number 2003103732

ISBN 0-9660449-7-5

Cover photograph by Thomas E. Eltzroth
Cover design by Lina Psoma

First published in 2003 by:
Cosmos Publishing Co., Inc.
P.O.Box 2255
River Vale, NJ 07675
Phone: 201-664-3494
Fax: 201-664-3402
e-mail: authors@greeceinprint.com
web site: greeceinprint.com

Printed in Greece

WITH ALL MY BREATH

Selected Poems

by

John Manesis

COSMOS PUBLISHING

ACKNOWLEDGMENTS

Several poems in this collection, a few in slightly different versions, originally appeared in the following publications:

Zone 3, Mediphors, Forkroads, Poetic License.
Black Creek Review, Footwork: Paterson Literary Review.
Dream International Quarterly, North Coast Review.
Wisconsin Review, Poetry Motel, Second Glance.
Creighton Window, Nebo, California State Poetry Quarterly.
Bay Area Poetry Coalition, Loonfeather, Opus Literary Review.
Minerva, Lake Region Review, Mayo Magazine.
Touched by Adoption by Green River Press.
The Cancer Poetry Project by Fairview Press.

My thanks to the editors.

TABLE OF CONTENTS

PART ONE

PART TWO

PART THREE

For Bess
For Mary, Stephanie, George, and Peter

PART ONE

As you set out for Ithaka,
hope your journey is a long one,
full of adventure, full of discovery...

C. P. Cavafy, *Ithaka*

SAM SPADE & CO.

As I wait in a long line
trading my lunch hour
for a book of Christmas stamps,
all of it comes back to me–
the hours my brother and I studied
Wanted posters on those drab walls–
mug shots of desperados
with five o'clock shadows–
murderers, arsonists, bank robbers.
We then ventured out into a city of danger,
confident we would soon claim
a fortune in reward money.
We followed one guy into the bank
only to discover he was the head teller.
Once two men were huddled on a corner
with their collars turned up–
we overheard the words "blast" and "armed"
and tailed the pair for an hour
until they faded into the smoke
of the Legion hall on Veterans Day.
In our greatest coup we uncovered a spy,
a swarthy little man with dark glasses
who emerged from the Albanian's
shoe shine shop with a white cane
and tapped his way down Main Street.
"Bullshit, he's faking," my brother insisted
so we took turns darting in front of him
but couldn't make him flinch.
We gave up and went home after we saw

him walk into a light pole.
The lady in front of me finally moves–
the ten year old boy beside her
turns and eyes me suspiciously–
I remove the shades,
put the black gloves in my pocket
and try to look nonchalant.

A UNIVERSAL LANGUAGE

When Aunt Katie was a child,
before she learned to speak English,
my grandmother told her in Greek
to go to the corner grocery
and buy a pound of ground beef.
Her finger thumping the table top,
she had her daughter repeat,
"amberget, amberget, amberget!"
Nudged out the door,
her hand wrapped around a dollar bill,
she measured each step to the store,
echoing that harsh word to herself
as if opening night awaited her,
the curtain about to be raised.
She went inside and sidled up
to the glass and there it was–
a mound of meat in a paper tray,
between the chicken and the chops.
The owner, arms folded,
towered above her, waiting...
but when she tried to speak
her tongue clung to the floor of her mouth.
He walked around the counter,
smiled and directed her to point.
She soon was racing home
as if her feet had wings,
a raven haired Nike hugging
a white package of victory.

SAVINGS

When I was a boy my elders,
survivors of the Great Depression,
advised me to save my money for a rainy day–
all but one, that is, my godfather,
who was the owner, patron saint,
and best customer of the Paradise Bar.
When I visited his smoky domain
and found him slouched on a bar stool,
he pried himself away from the dice,
a deck of cards, a bottle of Jack Daniels
and a dolly entrenched beside him.
He would pat me on the shoulder,
flash a gummy grin and wade
through his flock of motley regulars
to lift a five spot from the till,
holding the bill between nicotinic fingers
as if Abe Lincoln had just sprouted wings.
"Spend this! Don't save it! Have a good time!"
he insisted as he walked me to the door.
I spent the money like he told me to
but not all of it–
I saved a shiny coin for him
and made a deposit in my memory bank.
Whenever it looks like rain,
I borrow that silver dollar
and to hell with an umbrella.

THEA, THE STORY TELLER

I ran with her to the port
when her father returned from Corfu Town,
waving the sky blue scarf
he had promised to buy.

With her hands
I harvested the grapes,
heavy on the Ionian vines
and we drank of the red wine.

Through her eyes I saw
the priest, PappaYiannis,
buried beside the white church
where he had married,
where he had often sung Eonias,
the prayer of eternal memory.

So many stories,
armfuls of wood she gathered
on that small island to build a boat
laden with vinegar, spices, and olive oil.
Though she is gone now,
I still sail to Erikousa
and nearing that distant shore
lean over the stern, seeing myself
more clearly in the sea.

WHATEVER HAPPENED TO ZACK,

the only black man in town?
Coal colored face thrust forward,
his head gleaming like an eight ball,
he would stop us on the street,
pull out a gold pocket watch
that dangled from a long chain
and glittered like his front tooth.
He glanced at the time
and wide-eyed like a professor
quizzing his students asked,
"Boys, when's the two o'clock bus
gonna leave for Chipp'wa Falls?"
We stammered, shifted our feet
and answered, "Well...two o'clock."
"Natu'lly, natu'lly," he said,
chuckling while he walked away.

One night, at closing time,
a bartender found him,
dead in a tavern basement,
the back of his head gashed.
Some said it was an accident,
that he had fallen down the stairs,
but the gold watch he loved
so much had disappeared.
Whatever happened to Zack,
the only black man in town?

THE ICE MAN

When the sun is overhead,
hovering like a globe of fire,
and stillness blankets the afternoon,

I remember those aestival days
and rushing to an open truck
that trundled down a narrow street,

stopped in front of our house.
When we extended a neighborhood
of little hands, he chiseled an edge

with a long pick and supplied
a frosty treat to each of us.
And then he hefted the blocks,

grasping them with metal tongs,
his face and neck beaded with sweat
as he delivered the ice.

THE RIGHT TIME

Thirty years ago my cousin,
shackled by delusions and despair,
was taken to an asylum
on the island of Corfu,
not far from his birthplace.

A doctor asked him,
"What is your name?
Where were you born?
What day is it?"
When there was no answer,
the doctor scribbled a few lines
on a blank sheet of paper
and closed the chart.

Days passed into years, one brick
laid upon another, row on row,
and by the time four walls rose
above his head my cousin,
numbed by tranquilizers, had quit
bloodying his fists against the stone.

But every night, before he dropped
into a well of fitful sleep he pressed
an ear to the wall and listened
to the outside world he remembered—
the plaintive strings of a buzuki,
his mother humming in the kitchen,
wine glasses clinking in a cafenio.

[22]

After spending half his life confined,
he collapsed and in that final hour
as he was borne away looked upward,
saw a small square of blue sky and said,
"I know what day it is."

CITY PARK SUNDRIES

-for Nick Manesis

In a 50's style cafe,
while sipping coffee,
I hear a fork ping,
a malt machine is whirring–
my father's face appears
in the mirror behind the soda fountain,
his thinning hair combed back,
that dimpled chin and prominent nose,
the serious look–

"All right, let's get to work,"
he decreed in a less complicated age
of one man, one vote rule.
With sleeves rolled up,
a tie tucked into his shirt,
he handed aprons to my brother and me
when we reported for duty at that store
in Denver he had bought the week before.
We would have rather been playing baseball
but in our fifteenth summer began
to sweep the floors, stock the shelves
and squeegee the windows clean,
learned to make correct change
and mastered the cash register,
became veteran soda jerks,
concocting sundaes, malts, and shakes,
without, as our father put it,
"giving away the store."
"Yes, maam," and "No, sir,"

were etched in our lexicon
as we sold a medley of goods–
bottles of Kaopectate, Geritol,
Anacin and Pepto-Bismol,
packs of Pall Malls, Old Golds
and Luckies that went for 25 ¢,
Mail Pouch and Red Man tobacco
old timers wadded into chaws,
Ex-lax or Feenamint for customers
who insisted on being "regular,"
the Alka Seltzer discs that fizzed
away in bubbly glasses.
For men and boys who would be men
and wanted "rubbers" or "prophylactics,"
we discreetly dispensed Trojans or Ramses
and to the glee of eighteen year olds,
they could buy 3.2 beer to go,
including Sundays, as we hustled
to keep the coolers jammed with brands
like Coors and Falstaff, Tivoli and Hamms.

The footsteps of those who shared
that journey resonate in the halls
and corridors of memory–
the burly policeman, Leonard Johnson,
whose car rammed a tree on his last patrol,
an aging former boxer, Dempsey,
who heard the clang of phantom bells
as he lurched down the street,

Lee Hazelwood, the Cicero
of 21st and York, a cab driver
and ex-army officer whose dispatcher
is probably still trying to locate him,
Bobby Phelan with the auburn hair
and meteoric Irish temper,
the gentle Greek immigrant, old Angelo,
an employee whose candle burned down
on the cancer ward of the VA Hospital,
a wrinkled black man, George, who loved
King Edward cigars and charged them
until his monthly check arrived,
then always paid his bill to "Mr. Nick."

"Do you want a refill?...
Sir, would you like a refill?"
the teenage waitress asks.
I catch a final glimpse of him,
lay a hand over the cup
and say, "I wish I could."

ARSENI MANESIS

You see the way I am?
My strength is gone
and I can't walk no more–
the doctor calls my sickness MS.

I remember how it started–
1936 at your father's wedding.
No feeling in my right hand
and no matter how hard I try
I can't tie my own shoes so I ask
your aunt who does it for me.
She thought I made a joke.

Five years before I got sick
my friend, Nick, from same village
in Greece, came to Chicago and found
pretty young woman he wants to marry
but he already has wife and two boys
in old country waiting for him to come back.
He says to me, "Arseni, you stand up for me–
I need witness to say I am good man,
not married, that you know me from Greece.
Don't worry, they will believe you–
I make it up to you later on."
In front of God, I raised my right hand
but inside I knew it was wrong, a lie.
Funny thing, they were never happy,
never good for each other
and after two years she leaves him.

You see now how this happened,
why the sickness start in my right hand?
My own fault, nobody else.
God knows.

BIKER, 1976

The year of the bicentennial,
after months of wheeling myself into shape,
I, a gritty forty year old in a red T shirt,
black riding shorts and padded gloves,
headed east from Fargo into Minnesota
on a four hundred mile trek,
convinced that along the way
I would be interviewed
by a local TV station or newspaper.
That morning even the fields
of barley and sunflowers seemed to bristle
as I rode by and after thirty miles
coasted into a small town and stopped
at a place called Mom's Cafe.
While I sipped a can of pop at the counter
and looked at a map, a farmer seated nearby
with a thumb hooked on bib overalls
studied me from beneath a John Deere cap.
"Where ya headin'?" the oldster asked.
"Park Rapids. Can you tell me
which back road is the best?"
He ran a weathered index finger
over a line on the map
and ambled outside with me.
"That's seventy miles," he cautioned,
eying my ten speed as if it were
a two wheel version of an Edsel.
Puffed with pride, I breezily replied,
"No problem. See you later,"

took a running start on my bike
and swung my leg over the seat–
a pack draped over the back wheel
caught in the spokes–
I catapulted over the handlebars
and belly flopped on the gravel road.
Staggering to my feet, I dusted myself off
and prayed only the two of us had witnessed
the Flying Wallenda from North Dakota.
He gaped at me, gathered himself
and without a hint of sarcasm said,
"Not off to a very good start, are we?"
I pedalled down the street
like a thief sneaking out of town
and when I passed the Slow sign laughed
as hard as my sore ribs would allow,
soothed in knowing I wouldn't be stopping
at Mom's Cafe on the way back.

MY WARDROBE

I unwind a scarf of adverbs,
toss it to the side
and turn my coat inside out
in search of the proper noun.
I discard a shirt full of cliches
and empty all my pockets,
groping for the right verb.
By the time even a hint
of a metaphor rolls around
my clothes are on the floor
and I am standing in a corner
in the same old birthday suit.
When all seems lost I do
what I should have at the start–
close my eyes and try to *see*,
cover my ears and try to *hear*.

MIDNIGHT QUIZ

I often draw the same card
from my deck of dreams–
the joker, that wild man
who steals my pencil
just before the final exam,
sends me to the wrong class
or gives me a phony map
knowing I'll never pass
if I can't find the professor.
So there I am, shaking in my sleep
as I run around the campus,
having to play an inside straight
against a full house of agitation.
Will someone shuffle, please?

SOLO

I pushed her harder and harder–
"To Mars! To Jupiter! To Pluto!' I called out–
"Higher! Higher!" my daughter commanded,
her patent leather shoes
pointing to the stars–
"I'm flying to the moon!"
I let go and backed away, afraid–
she sped through space with windswept hair
and hands so small and white
clinging to the chains
until at last the empty swing
came to rest.

MY GRANDFATHER'S FAREWELL

The day of yiayia's funeral,
papouli sat quietly in the dining room.
Subdued voices and softened footsteps
filled the house and yet it seemed empty
as the extended family prepared itself
for the church ceremony.

"Are you coming, Pa?" my aunt asked.
He swept his palm along the table top
and answered in Greek,
"Poteh etsi tha teen itho"–
"Never will I see her that way."
No one tried to change his mind.

We closed the door behind us
and left him with his memories
of their long and fruitful marriage,
a resurrection of a moving play
whose scenes were never staged,
the opening lines in Koroni, Greece,
the curtain fall in Rockford, Illinois.

TORNADO JOE

The seventy year old bachelor,
bundled in clothes that reeked
and draped in a tattered coat,
patrolled the downtown,
toting a bucket and squeegee
to clean the merchants' windows.

In 1957, after a tornado roared
through the city and killed a family,
he told anyone who would listen
that he had known it was coming–
"I felt it inside me," he insisted,
and for the next twenty years
often paused at the glass panes,
looking over his shoulder to cast
a wild and fearsome eye at the sky.
Some people teased him and asked,
"Joe, what do you see up there,
what are you looking at?"

One day his real name appeared
in the newspaper, a few terse lines
buried in the obituary column.
No, the second tornado never came–
at least not one the rest of could see.
But who knows how many times
during the turbulence of his days
he sighted a twisted cloud
as it threatened above the trees.

In his longest hours, how often
did the wind fall away to nothingness,
did the leaves stop fluttering?

DOWNTOWN ON CHRISTMAS DAY

While I wait at a stop light,
sorting out my holiday plans,
a young woman, nicely dressed,
trudges toward me on the snowy walk
with her head down and a gray scarf
streaming behind her.

When she glances up at me
her eyes are dark and steady–
I look the other way.
The light changes and she grows
smaller in the rear view mirror,
merging with the empty street.
The Red River ahead, glazed with ice,
looms larger than yesterday.

NIGHTFALL AT PALM SPRINGS

Accustomed to the way
a prairie horizon portrays
the fading edge of day,
I marvel at the scene—
the sun, poised atop the crest
of the San Jacinto range,
recedes behind the summit,
the radiance waning toward the sea.
The azure color above softens
and the rock upheaval darkens
beneath a rising layer of light.
The foothills, tinged in green,
merge with ridges, brown and beige,
and at higher elevations the snow,
shadowed clefts and pines coalesce,
a fusion of hues and lines.
The sierra becomes a silhouette
as evening advances and draws
a veil of stars across the heaven's face.
Enfolded, the mountains, sky, and I are one.

YEARNING

During lulls in the restaurant,
the waitress lingered at my table,
close enough for me
to reach out and touch.
Attractive and trim,
about my daughter's age,
she spoke of her teenage son
who would soon be leaving home,
the demands of being a single parent
and her desire to return to college.
She hesitated at times
in the middle of a sentence,
as if words were left unsaid.

One day she told me
she wanted to buy a home.
"Don't let them sell you a place
you can't afford," I cautioned,
then a little sheepishly added,
"Sorry, I sound like a father."
She stared at me
and smiled wistfully
as though a sudden breeze
had whished through her window,
parting curtains she had drawn.
"That's all right," she said,
"I never had a father."

THE KEEPSAKE

-for Thea Kati

The lemon tree she grew from seed
and nurtured with wrinkled hands
beside a window in her house
stands tall in my solarium.
A woody rind encircles older stems,
while upward, at the skylight dome,
the newer branches finger toward the sun.
I rub the ovate leaves between my palms,
inhaling a tangy scent so different
than any other plant of mine.
Who can say with certainty
this tree will ever bear a single fruit?
But even if that never comes to be,
what I have savored lives on
in blossoms and the boughs,
within the deepest roots.

JEWEL

The storm has passed.
I daydream on the redwood deck,
oblivious of the westward sun,
an amber sphere about to disappear
behind a row of silver maple trees.

A drop of rain, suspended from
a leaf of marigold nearby,
refracts a ray of light
and rouses me from reverie.
With the slightest change of view,
this iridescent orb becomes
an opal, ruby, or an emerald.

RISING

At a long day's end
I was in darkness
until a blush of orange appeared,
a halo above the pines across the lake,
glowing like a distant fire
low in the southern sky.
Soon the full moon welled up,
and mirrored on the water
as a shimmering ribbon of light,
ascended in the summer night.

REGINA

Strange that my wife's cat,
having pretended for years
that I was a lamp or a hat,
deigns to be near me now
in the sunset of her reign.

She sidles up to me,
purrs loudly and turns
in small circles to rub one side
and then the other against my leg.
Still spry, this white fluff
springs up onto my lap,
settles, and kneads me with her paws.

I stroke her back,
raising static tufts of long hair,
and I am flattered–
imagine me about to be allowed entry
into the royal courtyard–
but as I try to hold her she stiffens,
fixes me in an azure gaze of ice,
and when she leaps down,
the palace gates swing shut.

MY GLOVE

Once or twice a year,
while boys are shagging balls
in the park across the street,
I, a middle aged Ponce de Leon,
rummage through the garage,
foundering in a sea of boxes.
At last I find my glove
and ease it on as I always do,
pound the pocket with my fist
and tell myself I could play today–

but I want to remember
Joe Dimaggio the way
he raced from first to third,
his graceful outfield style
and power at the plate.
Let someone else watch
an idol hobble around the bases
in an Old Timers Game.
So I return my glove to its proper place,
to be retrieved whenever I see
a ball that's spinning toward me
from my summer days.

IN A ROOM UPSTAIRS

-for Yiayia

When my grandmother struck a match
and lit a candle next to the icon,
the coat hanging in the corner
no longer resembled an intruder.

She sat beside me on the bed
and murmured a prayer in Greek,
only part of which I understood,

crossed herself and made the same sign
on my forehead and hands,
her fingertips warm and steady.

Not having to say anything else,
she returned to the kitchen
and I fell asleep listening to
the sound of her slippered feet.

I don't remember what ailed me–
some fifty years have passed–
and yet whenever I summon her,

she ascends the stairs,
the candle still glows,
soft and low, and her light
brightens my darkest nights.

A WINDING OF STILL WATER

Voices, low but clear,
carry across water–
I see a man and two boys
and the reflection of fading light
from their white boat.
I lift the anchor and drift–

before we left the dock,
our uncle, trying to look serious,
turned toward my brother and me
and asked,"Boys, who's the boss?"
"You are, Theo Yioryi," we said.
He plied the rickety oars
and guided us through a passage,
a winding of still water
between the reeds and lily pads.
We came to our favorite place,
hooked slippery minnows and lofted them
with cane poles toward a solitary stump.
While we waited,
I scooped a handful of lake
and saw it trickle through my fingers.
The corks began to bob and twitch
and soon we filled a bucket
with sunfish, crappies, and perch
and all the while our uncle kept
the lines untangled and a space
open for each of us.

Green has turned to gray–
the lake is a mirror.
I make just one more cast
toward a different stump
and watch the ripples disappear.
The rod and reel feel
heavy in my hand–
not a nibble, not a bite.
I head for the far shore
without a fish but my creel is full.

PART TWO

And if the soul
Is to know itself,
it must look
into a soul...

George Seferis, *Mythistorema*

HOUDINI'S METAMORPHOSIS

An unlikely beginning–
a short and muscular mother's boy
dared to leave home at any early age,
a Jewish Hungarian immigrant
who borrowed a French magician's name
and added a vowel to make it sound Italian.
He spent years enclosed
in dime museums and beer halls
before learning to free himself
from his fetters and handcuffs,
emerging finally at center stage.

He held his breath long enough
to bubble up from watery coffins,
survived the Milk Can Act
and the Chinese Water Torture,
with ankles bound dangled upside down
high above a sea of faces,
wriggling out of straight jackets–
a life of illusions and escapes.

But one night while children
in ghostly sheets and death masks
scurried around the block swinging
jack-o-lanterns grinning light,
he heard a spirited knock at
his door and a voice called out,
"Trick of treat?"

"Trick," Houdini managed to reply.
He listened to the skeleton key
click in the lock, the knob turned
and his chains clattered to the floor.

THE WATCH

I am the fire
you hope will soon consume itself,
blazing in the distant hills.

I am the flames
raging at someone else's door.

I am the smoke
ascending from the ruins.

I am the embers
that glow in never ending nights.

I am the ashes
that won't be swept away
and if it takes a hundred years
I will renew myself.

I am
Sarajevo.

REFLECTION

Naked,
the teenager stands
sideways before a mirror,
ignoring her mother's pleas
at the bedroom door.

She cranes to inspect
the shrivelled breasts and studies
her ribs, flared as a swan's back.
With one hand on her spine,
the other against her abdomen,
she measures herself.

When she turns to face
the reflection in the glass,
she remembers the carnival,
the low and narrow corridor
and other girls laughing
at contorted faces and wide torsos.

She hears the last meal–
a bite of an apple–
churning above the navel
like water on the rise.

GRAVEN IMAGES

"I no longer wanted to be an artist."
Beto de la Rocha, *L.A. Times*

The painter slashed every canvas,
smashed the wooden frames
and torched his life's work
as though his soul was afire.
"But why?" his friends asked–
"Because I loved my art
more than God," he explained
and withdrew from the world.

For twenty years he searched
the Scriptures for an answer,
memorizing verse after verse.
When he lay upon the cot
and closed his weary eyes,
mad Nebuchadnezzar appeared,
babbling in the fields,
clouds of locusts swirled into Egypt,
Job's sores and blisters wept.

One night, deep in a chasm,
pressed against the dank walls,
over and over he yelled
for someone to raise him up
but the only sounds he heard
were the echoes of his own voice.
He understood what he had to do
and began the steep ascent,

inching upward, his swathed hands
clawing at the earth's mossy bones–
the dirt, stones, rocks, bare roots.

He awoke then,
drew back the shades
and waited at the window.
Morning finally came,
a garden of hues on the horizon
blazing with lilacs, roses, and blues
and as he watched the sun rise
relived the light in his landscapes.
The painter took up his brush again.

GORGEOUS GEORGE

1950
LA
A morning star
at the dawn of television
sashays down the aisle
with golden tresses caressing an orchid robe,
heralded by the clarion chords
of Pomp and Circumstance.
As his valet perfumes the ring,
the wrestler swishes through the ropes,
revelling in the swell of hisses and boos.
The lifted eyebrow
pounds of feigned indignation
slugs of flim flam
hammer locks
half Nelsons
wrist flicks
body slam
one two three
raised fist
empty arena
lights out
1963

YOUR SOLARIUM

While your husband and children sleep,
you throw off your heavy blanket,
tiptoe down the hall and enter
that secret parlor where no ray
of outer light has ever shone.
Trailing vines of philodendron
and bracts of bougainvillea
brush against your flushed cheek
as you ease the glass door open
and remove the statuette,
holding your breath–
how many times have you imagined her
slipping through your fingers,
shattering on the terra cotta tiles?
As you cradle her against your breast
and caress the swirls of her gown,
the fragrance of ceramic roses
in her flawless hand fills you.
Even in the dark you know that face–
fingertips have memorized the almond eyes,
high cheekbones, the delicate brow.
You return her to your hiding place,
vowing anew that she will someday
exit the room with you.

GRETA

Had you removed
the dark glasses and slouch hat,
had you lingered, then spoken
on those misty days along the boulevard,
would Camille's sculptured face
have looked the same?
Would there have been the magic
in the ballerina's voice?
The one who told the world,
I want to be
alone.

WILL YOU PAY THE PRICE?

No one could explain what happened then
to all the children living in this town.
The mountainside that parted, claiming them,
would never gape again. Did any drown,
succumb on lofty peaks to ice and snow,
were they sold or bartered into slavery?
How many survived and do their offspring know
about this tale of wonder and of misery?

If in the night your children speak low
and linger by the door on restless feet,
or ask of you how far the rivers flow,
should they be drawn to music in the street,
stop what you are doing, listen long–
what you hear may be the piper's song.

ODE TO "WRONG WAY" CORRIGAN

Having been denied permission
several times to fly your "crate"
across the Atlantic, you told
authorities as you left New York
that July day in 1938
you were returning to Long Beach.
Twenty-nine hours later your monoplane
touched down near Dublin, Ireland.
You claimed to have been lost,
that it was all a "mistake,"
and with a choir boy's innocent smile
explained to disbelieving reporters
how both compasses had gone awry.
Never mind you flew due east
when you lifted off the runway,
that at times the ocean
must have glimmered beneath your wings.
A hero, you sailed back to America
to a ticker tape parade
that would have made a President blush.
For the rest of your days,
you had to have relished that moniker,
delighted in retelling the story.
Wherever you're headed this time,
we'll down a glass or two
of Irish brew for you.

PUBLIC DEFENDER

Distinguished members of this avian jury,
the bird before your beaks, *Passer domesticus*,
could not have harbored such an awful fury,
would never have perpetrated a crime so vicious.
Not a feather of evidence, a forced confession,
sensational headlines in the Jailbird Gazette,
the usual witnesses that sing in unison,
the coroner, a flighty, inexperienced vet.

While Cock Robin's killer is flying high,
my client's caged, indicted for this deed
because the prosecutor needs a fall guy,
a member of an overpopulated breed–
the sad familiar tale of a common sparrow,
an immigrant who was framed by a bloody arrow.

REHEARSAL

With the lights low,
she glances at the mirror
as though it were an audience,

tells herself,
I know my lines by heart–
a little more makeup now

and I can go to the store.
When he comes home,
he'll hand me a bouquet,

a card with the right poem,
and we'll be passionate tonight.
He shouldn't have done it–

if someone asks why this happened,
I will remember what to say,
the part that I'm supposed to play.

I'll give him one more chance–
deep down I know he loves me
the way he always has.

THE GIFT

One would have assumed
she viewed the world
in a limited way,
standing by the window
of that Amherst house
where for many years
she had confined herself.
But at her writing table,
she discarded trappings
of ribbons, bows
and ornamental wrappings,
reached inside
and held each word
in abeyance until
the vision of the poem
revealed itself to her.
By then, a universe
had entered the room—
the gift endowed to Emily
when she was just a child.

BY THE WAYSIDE

At a T shaped intersection,
a mile from the nearest house,
a rusty pickup pulled off the road
and stopped before a wooden cross.
A young woman stepped down
and laid an artificial wreath
of red roses on the memorial.
The companion, about her age,
sat gripping the steering wheel,
his forehead pressed against his hands.
She gazed at the name inscribed
as she stood on the desert sand,
framed by the San Gorgonio peaks
to the west, their snowy crowns
basking in the noon day sun.
He soon called out to her
and when they drove away,
the truck looked like a mirage
in the distance, shimmering
as it rolled down the highway,
past the the palms and sagebrush,
past the flowering brittlebush.

I WAS A SODA JERK

and had a part time job
across the street from Hollywood High.
Julia Turner used to stop in
and I was crazy about her,
a gorgeous blonde in the same grade
who never seemed to notice me.
I was working up the nerve
to ask her to go to the show
but whenever she sat at the counter,
leaned over in that tight sweater
and batted her eyes, I'd forget
what I was supposed to say.
One day she came into the malt shop,
said she had cut typing class
and wanted one of my sundaes.
I gave her an extra scoop of vanilla,
added plenty of chopped nuts,
squirted on the whip cream
and plopped two cherries on top.
She started wetting her lips
and I said to her, "Julia"–
that was her name then,
she changed it to Lana later–
"Julia, I been thinking..."
"Yes, Johnnie," she purred, "About what?"
But before I could even answer
a guy from one the newspapers
who was giving her the eye
moved over and sat next to her.

He introduced himself and asked,
"You want to be in the movies?"
"I don't know, I'll have to ask my mother."
She gave him her telephone number,
told him to call in a few days
and was out the door.
I paid the dime for the sundae
and ate it myself, thinking
about her the whole time,
rehearsing what I was going to say
when she came in again.
But that was the last I saw of her
until she showed up on the screen
the next year, 1937, in a movie called,
"They Won't Forget"–
as if I ever could.

GREEN THUMB

He went to market to sell our cow, did Jack–
and what do you think that he brought back?
A handful of beans! I threw them out the window–
what can I do with him? I'm just a widow
and here we are, down to our last shilling.
I scold him all the time–why's he willing
to trust the people peddling poppycock?
Those beans are worthless as a worn out sock.

When Mother's mad at me, I wait until
she's gone to bed and come and sit real still
in the garden where I know each plant so well
and listen to every story that they tell.
*I can't **make** things grow, I **let** them grow.*
Sshh, it's coming up — I told you so.

VENTRILOQUIST

Edgar Bergen, formal and aloof,
unsure of his own appeal,
invented Charlie McCarthy,
the monocled sidekick who sat
on the "belly talker's" right
sporting a top hat and tails.
With Bergen as his prop,
how sharp the dummy was,
his verbal barbs lancing the likes
of Bill Fields and Mae West
who jousted with him
at the pinnacle of radio days.
The repartee with his creator, though,
endeared him most to audiences
with cocky lines like the ones
he cackled in mock belligerence,
"I'll *mow* ya down, Bergen,
so help me, I'll *mow* ya down."

When the entertainer folded up
his wooden friend at the end
of the performance, Charlie cried,
"Oh, no, not the trunk again!"
His partner locked away,
did Bergen, in moments of solitude,
regret not having nurtured his
own voice, not having called up
more often the most vulnerable words,
the hardest ones to say?

HOW FAR

Enough of bunts and pitcher's duels–
the fans jammed the parks to cheer
the former ace of the Bosox staff
who became a Yankee outfielder,
the home run king
with his all or nothing swing.
The Babe often fanned,
his heavy torso spinning
on spindly legs into a pinstriped coil
but when the slugger launched the ball
and it soared into the summer blue,
a roar erupted from the stands
and the crowd was on its feet.

The twenties–
the long ball era had begun
and throngs found someone to idolize,
a man-child with a moon face and fondness
for mischief, cigars, and camel hair caps.
He helped them forget a recent World War,
Prohibition, and the Black Sox Scandal,
reminded them that if a scruffy boy
could journey from the dusty field
of St. Mary's Industrial School
and star in the big leagues,
who is to say how far
they too could travel.

FREED

Fear, a constant companion,
dogged the boy to school,
snapping at his pant legs–
called upon in class to speak
the more he fractured words,
the more protracted the pauses,
the more consonants clung to his larynx,
baffles in turbulent streams of air–

and so his voice inverted,
deeper than the swirls and coils
of his inner ear but when he dreamed
he saw himself seated in a great hall,
the teacher aiming a finger at him–
as the schoolboy rose,
classmates leaned forward, hushed–
he uncupped his hands and freed
a swallow that swept around the room
until it found a window
open to the world of sound.

GONE

On a deserted platform
beside the railroad station,
the old man stares up
at the still black hands
of the clock that faces west
high atop the depot tower.

A VISION

The villagers said he was a "crazy one,"
a codger compensated for his chores
not in silver coins but apple cores.
Meandering in the fields, his day was done
when he had planted all his well earned pay.
Then he laid his head upon the earth,
his bed, and unconcerned about his worth,
foresaw the harvest of another day.

Who remembers the parson's oratory,
the judge's proclamation, the banker's story?
Each spring, the blossoms, to everyone's delight,
adorn the countryside in pink and white.
And with the coming of the fruit, indeed
the children speak of Johnny Appleseed.

HERO

When first we met at the festival,
I was a maiden, innocent and demure,
dedicated to the priestess, Aphrodite,
but what did I know of love's allure?

Standing on this precipice at Sestos
above the stormy sea and rocky shores,
I lift my torch and pray for your return,
awaiting those arms, the golden oars

that nightly churn the Hellespont.
Leander, it is best we do not know
how long the gods have fated it to last,
this passion that consumes us so.

Are we beguiled by evenings past,
must a light that burns so brightly
soon spend itself? Does it portend
a tragic end for you and me?

We live in only half the world,
the one where darkness reigns,
as if we are a pair of prisoners
forever bound by custom's chains.

The fire is but a flickering flame—
again and again I shout your name.
Our destinies are intertwined
and if by heaven or hell's design,
Poseidon claims you for his own tonight,
can I endure the morning's telling light?

UNFORGETTABLE

After killing a trainer and escaping from a circus,
an elephant named Tyk was shot on a busy street.
Honolulu, AP Press, August 21, 1994

"Why did she go berserk?"
the veterinarian mused,
probing several of the bullet holes
as he circled the carcass,
studying it from trunk to tail.

He excised the eyes,
gazed at them under a microscope
and saw not the savanna's wide sky
but flashes from a thousand cameras
imprinted on the retinae.

He lifted the huge pinnae,
listened at the ear holes
and heard not the song of the wind
along the Serengeti but the sounds
of cymbals crashing and balloons
popping like a rifle regiment.

He cut away the ribs,
descended into the depths
of the thoracic cage and there
discovered the last birthday cake,
shaped like an elephant's heart,
the icing topped with peanut butter
and twenty-one carrot sticks.

[75]

PART THREE

Well, it was found that the gold of the olive root had dripped into the leaves of his heart...

Odysseus Elytis, *The Autopsy*

A BEGINNING

The anatomy professor
ushered our student retinue
into the large dissection room
as light slanted through the windows
that autumn afternoon.

Bespectacled and reverent,
he called our names and assigned
a foursome to each cadaver
where we, the acolytes, would serve
the coming year at medicine's altar.

After initial anxious moments,
we lifted up our instruments
that gleamed in halos of suspended lamps
to study muscles, nerves, vessels and bones–
the covers and bindings of their books.

Since then I've come to ask myself
about the missing words and sentences,
the blank pages of their days.
Where did their travels take them,
did anyone record their stories?
How many went unclaimed,
who among them willed away the last,
perhaps the only thing they owned?

WEN

The first time we made rounds
as junior medical students
at the Omaha V.A. Hospital,
we crowded behind Dr. Kleitch,
a handful of foot soldiers
in the company of a General.
The conversations on the ward
came to a halt in mid-sentence
as he made his entrance,
a compact surgeon with grey hair
that bristled, wire rimmed glasses
and eyes glinting like ball bearings.
He stopped to examine a patient
who dangled his feet over the bed.
Dr. Kleitch pointed to a lump
on the man's forehead and asked me,
"What's that, Doctor?"
I stared at the swelling,
hoping in vain it would somehow
reveal its mysteries to me,
and replied, "I don't know."
"You don't know? I am sure even
he knows," the surgeon proclaimed,
glaring at the patient who gulped,
cleared his throat and said,
"Sorry, me neither, Doc."
I thought I saw a faint smile
trying to escape from the corner
of our leader's mouth.

"It's a wen...spelled, W.E.N.,
a sebaceous cyst, Doctors,
benign, well circumscribed,
non-tender, soft, and commonly seen
on the face, scalp or back.
Don't ever forget it!"
I survived that initiation,
my boot camp, with a flesh wound
but no internal injuries.
To this day, whenever I see a wen,
the curtains of the past part,
Dr. Kleitch strides onto the stage
and there I am in the front row,
lucky to have a ticket to the show.

TREMOR

The young adult, hunched in a chair,
fists on his knees, queried me,
"Why does every pipe I grab
at work turn to rust the next day?
When I asked Doc Lemay,
he laughed at me," the man said,
his eyes like grey stones
at the bottom of a cold creek.
Selecting words the way
an expert in explosives
handles a suspicious package,
I explained the composition of sweat,
delayed effects of humidity,
the way that metals oxidize–
a solemn oration of gibberish.
An eerie calm came over him
and his hands fell to his side.
Nodding, he left the office
and I never saw him again.
Now, twenty five years later,
I wonder if he felt the rumble,
the fault lines shifting in his life,
if I should have helped him see
the cracks angling beneath his feet
instead of running for safer ground.

A PSYCHIATRIC OPINION

Why do you need to sit atop the wall,
ignoring all the dangers that are involved?
There are some other patients, I recall,
who've lived on the edge and never have resolved
their inner conflicts. This nonconformity
is a compulsive trait, a form of obsession,
perhaps a rebellion against authority–
as a child, were you forced to go to confession?

If you should tumble down from such a height,
consider the spectacle, a gruesome sight–
who would want to gather up the pieces?
Not even the King with all of his resources
could help you then. I recommend hypnosis,
a cure for many forms of psychoneurosis.

A NEW MAN?

Local tavern owners took up a collection
and purchased a kidney for him–
what bliss! He fared so well
he once again could down a six pack
and not get up at night to piss.

When his own heart failed,
pounding wildly against his chest,
the Society of Spare Parts
donated one that lulled him
to sleep with slow and steady beats.

Corneal transplants followed,
reversing dimness brought on
by years of leering at every skirt in town–
his peepers became so keen he could spot
a set of knockers half a block away.

But after he had a stroke
and his brain was replaced,
he drank warm milk instead of booze,
paid no attention to his pulse,
ogled books instead of babes
and asked the addled strangers around him,
"Are you sure you have the right person?"

THE HOME

An aide draws all the shades,
an orderly dims all the lights,
someone shuffles down the hall,
somebody mumbles behind a door.

BIRTHDAY

As you always do
the day before Christmas,
you open the scrapbook
to a familiar headline
in an old newspaper clipping–
"Baby Jane Doe, a newborn,
abandoned at local hospital."
Beneath the caption, a picture of her
with tiny fingers reaching out,
her mouth a bawling circle.
You pat the face on the page
as though to quiet the infant,
as though to reassure her.
The story still overwhelms you–
snowy footprints that holiday eve,
the surprised nurse who found her
in a box inside the back door,
the note pinned to her blanket.
You linger over the details,
longing for the lost pieces
in the puzzle of a life
that began thirty years ago.
You close the scrapbook
but the same questions haunt you–
if you ever find your mother,
will she want to see you?
Who are you?
Why?

THE DYING MAN

The entourage that fills the room
probes and sounds the dying man
and all his divisible parts
are claimed and accounted for.

The first chants an incantation,
reaches deeply into his bag
and removes a vial of mystic cells.
He says, "It's blood he needs."

The second grasps a golden knife,
holds it high for all to see
and sweeps it through the air.
He says, "Out with his spleen."

The third peers into the inner eye,
finds a single thread and tugs,
unravelling a clew of dreams.
He says, "Dementia, don't you see?"

When they depart,
the dying man lifts his heart,
holds each chamber to his ear
and wrapped in a white sheet,
rises and begins to dance.

THE MARROW'S MEMORY

I have seen the X-rays
of those children's bones–
cracked and bowed extremities,
zigzag skull fractures,
displaced growth plates,
the broken clavicles and ribs.

I have seen the shrouds
of calcium being laid down,
the new bone that wraps
around the sites of injury
as skeletons mend themselves.
After many weeks, the evidence
of trauma usually disappears
and the bones seem whole again.

But I can not see
in any shadows before me
the marrow's memory,
the soul within the bones
that never forgets
the fist and boot,
the kicks and blows.

LEADING LADY

The couple exited the cafe,
the woman, straight and tall,
with a crown of silver hair.
Her gloved hand at his elbow,
along the avenue they came
beneath a basilica of trees.
She nodded as they passed–
the distance between us grew
and I heard the city claim
the rhythmic click of heels,
the fading shuffle of shoes.

CAREER CHOICES

My friends have asked
if I went into medicine
because of the prestige,
was it to help mankind,

did research interest me?
These were considerations
but I have a confession to make–
the real reason was Roger Borovoy.

In the sixth grade after class,
we had a fist fight – my first and last.
While I peppered him with jabs
and showed off my fancy footwork,

a vision of the middleweight champ,
Tony Zale, flashed before me
and I was certain that
the boys pressed in around us

were witnessing an epic bout.
Roger Borovoy, short and squat,
pawed the floor with a heavy boot
and waited for an opening–

like Jake Lamotta, the raging bull,
he lowered his head and charged,
knocked me on my ass
and pummelled me with lefts and rights.

Had my brother not yanked him off,
my noggin would still be bouncing
on the floor of the Normal School.
I trudged home with a puffy lip,

a case of damaged pride,
and told my skeptical father
I had run into a couple of boards,
neglecting to mention

they were inside a pair of fists.
Why did I become a doctor?
Whenever someone asks,
I smile and rub my lower lip,
aware of how I would have fared
in another line of work.

FOND REMEMBRANCE

I was walking down a corridor
in the clinic where I work
when the pair of elderly ladies
in front of me stopped.
One peered at a photograph
in a row of pictures on the wall
and as she studied the bald pate
and wrinkled visage of a deceased doctor,
I imagined she was remembering
a miraculous cure of long ago,
perhaps an all night vigil
at the bedside of her relative
when house calls were commonplace,
maybe years of faithful service
he had provided the community.
Pointing a bony finger at the frame,
she turned to her friend,
thumped a cane on the floor
and announced, "That's the one
that just about did Vernon in."

MEDITERRANEAN SUNSET

Born in Italy by the sea,
the spinster who taught for years
on a barren North Dakota plain
possessed the manner and look
of a schoolmarm, I thought–
so formal and dispassionate,
her brunette hair pulled back,
a pair of delicate bifocals
perched on a narrow nose.
The final time I visited her,
while searching for words
that might allay her pain,
the end of a conversation
drifted into the hospital room–
two women reminiscing in the hall
about their former beaus.
One confessed, "I don't know
what I ever saw in him.
He was a waste of time."
When their busy voices faded away,
the lady from Anzio said,
"I never spoke that way
about the men I knew.
I loved them all,
everyone of them."
Her face blossomed as if
a wild and solitary rose
had suddenly bloomed
within a fallow field.

Finally, I could see
what had always been before me—
she set her glasses aside,
reached up, untied her hair
and let it tumble
to her bared shoulders.

RESCUED

I was an intern
called to the pediatric ward
to see a two year old
in respiratory distress,
teetering on her elbows and knees,
wheezing and cyanotic.
The nurse had readied a tray
in the event of a tracheotomy,
a procedure I had never performed
in an adult, let alone a child.
Suddenly, the girl toppled forward
and stopped breathing.
The nurse handed me a scalpel,
ran to the phone and had the operator
page the surgical resident on call–
"Dr. Wilson, Dr. Wilson,
Stat, Room 121, Stat, Room 121!"
I stood motionless,
terrible moments ticking away,
the knife shiny and surreal,
clutched in a hand that seemed
to belong to someone else.
Dr. Wilson charged in,
grabbed the scalpel
and jumped onto the bed,
straddling the girl as he cut
an opening in the trachea
and slipped a tube inside.
"Breathe! Breathe!" he yelled,

compressing and releasing her chest
as if it were a small accordion.
At last, a gasp–
a tide of air
swished through the tube
and she began to breathe again,
those rhythmic sounds a haunting melody
I've heard a hundred times since then.

THE SUMMER SOLSTICE

You showed me the mammogram
and pointed to a white star
in the dark sky of my breast–
how innocent and far away it seemed,
a sparkle on the horizon,
but I could tell that you, stargazer,
had seen that heavenly sign many times.
When you excised the cancer,
no bigger than a fingertip,
I saw the red glare of my incision,
a half moon reflected in your glasses.
No need to remove my breast, you said–
had you done so how could I have filled
the emptiness, the darkness of space?
Heal my wound the way Heracles
had his charioteer, Iolaus,
seal the gashes of Hydra.
I need your magic,
not your strength.

THE WIDOW SPEAKS

Doctor, thank you
for taking care of my husband.
We trusted you and understood
whatever could be done was done.
You did explain the chemotherapy,
detailed the possible side effects,
discussed survival rates–
so professional, so complete.
I'm sure that everything
you said was true
but isn't there a way that you
can tell a man he's dying
and still leave him with hope?

MALE MENOPAUSE

The signs were unmistakable–
the acquaintance, long a steady soul,
raided his pension fund to buy
a flaming red Corvette,
began to flaunt gold chains,
auditioned for a hair transplant,
praying the tufts around his ears
would impress the dermatologist.
Instead of pizza and beer for lunch
he ordered veggie snacks,
enlisted in the Y brigade
and wheezed around the block,
attempting to deflate a pair of spares.
As for his wife, who raised their kids
and helped pay off his college bills,
he said, "No spark there anymore"–
leaving us to wonder who needed flint.
Divorce pending, he cavorted
with a pony tailed secretary
who graduated in his daughter's class.
But something happened on the way
to Cabo San Lucas and Mazatlan–
he maxed out his credit cards,
his senorita dumped him for Jose,
a guitarist in a mariachi band,
and when he called home collect,
his wife suggested he stay in Tijuana.
He did return and when I saw him last
was dining alone beneath a golden arch
on two Big Macs and a sack of fries,
his banged up Chevy in the parking lot.

DOLLY'S WOES

"The DNA in her cells shows telltale signs of wear."
The Associated Press

Nobody bothered me until last year.
I munched away in the fields,
not worrying about a thing,
feeling pretty because the guys
were giving me the look.
But then Doc Jitter, our vet,
started poking me for blood
and whispering to his pals.
Three months ago, over the hill,
before I could even say baaa
I was surrounded by a herd,
reporters clicking cameras,
and right behind then a bunch
of professor types ran around
like they were nuts and yelled,
"Dolly, you're a clone!"
They put my picture in the paper
and said that I might live forever
but no one bothered to ask
if that was OK with me.
At first I liked the attention
but changed my mind real quick.
The gals are jealous now
and none will chew the cud with me.
I got no privacy, can't even pee
without some jerk standing guard.
My Rambo found another squeeze–

he couldn't stand the fuss
whenever he came to see me
and says I ain't frisky anymore.
This sheep is feeling old.

FROM THE EARTH ITSELF

Sunrise.
Why am I standing here,
in this valley where
a generation ago I saw
so many of you fall and where
your blood was washed away,
your faces white as snow?

I could not find you
in public places, in the stones
and monuments, and still I dream
of bones piled high and ask myself
why our swords were forged
so proudly on our fathers' anvils.

And by tomorrow, what will come
of all the promises made today?
Who will stoke the fires
and who will shape the blades?
At last, here where the trumpets blew,
I hear you in the wind that stirs,
the litany of your whispered names
arising from the earth itself.

A FIFTIETH ANNIVERSARY INTERVIEW

-for the Navy flight nurses

Where shall I begin?

I was a small town girl
who had never been out of Wisconsin
until I graduated from high school.
The farthest I had travelled
was to a basketball tournament in Madison
as a cheerleader my senior year.
When the bus rolled into the capital
I was amazed at the number of people.

Medicine always interested me–
my uncle was a country doctor
who practiced forty years in Sawyer County.
I will never forget the first time
he let me look into his black bag
when I was a child. How fascinating–
listening to my heart
after he placed a stethoscope on my chest
and when he checked his own blood pressure
I watched the needle rise, then fall.
How I giggled when he made my knee
jump with a small reflex hammer.
I would have loved to become a doctor
but remember in those days
what was expected of women.

When I finished nursing school,
the thought of going overseas to care

[103]

for our troops sounded so romantic.
My father told me not to enlist–
he said it was too dangerous
but a twenty-one year old girl
doesn't worry about what might go wrong.
He gave me the gold chain and cross
that belonged to my grandmother–
you see, I'm still wearing it.

For flight nurses training
the Navy sent us to Alameda, California,
and afterwards flew us to Hawaii
and from there we went to Guam
where they had set up a tent hospital.
We made several flights to Iwo Jima,
a place I had never heard of until
we received our final orders.
The corpsman showed where it was
on the map of the western Pacific.
When we flew in on my first trip,
I looked over the pilot's shoulder
and as the island came into view
he pointed to Mt. Suribachi–
it reminded me of a great pyramid
that was rising out of a blue desert.
Could anyone have guessed how famous
that mountain would become?

We landed on a small air strip,
surrounded by casualties,
but could only jam two dozen litters
of the injured into the C47.
All we had to treat the marines
were Sulfa and Morphine,
units of blood, bandages and dressings–
and a plane full of prayers.
The corpsman and I worked together–
I wouldn't have made it without him.
We did our best for them
but how could anyone have been
prepared for what we saw?

Young men, some of them boys, really,
with head wounds, shrapnel injuries
to the chest and abdomen,
burns that blistered and oozed,
limbs that were shredded.
I knew some of the extremities
could not be saved but always told
the wounded we had the best surgeons
in the world waiting for them–
at times it's better to keep
part of the truth within you.

On one flight in March of 1945
two of the air lifted men died
but I left their faces uncovered
and went on talking to them
like I did all the others,
not wanting anyone to give up.
The survivors didn't discover
what had happened until we arrived
in Guam and unloaded the plane.
They held my hand then,
hugged me and thanked me.

I had the same dream
over and over again–
the war had ended and we nurses
were riding a night train home.
The radio was playing my favorite song,
Doris Day singing, "Sentimental Journey."
But then her voice trailed away
and when I looked out the window and saw
the way the lights were flashing by
I realized the train was speeding backward.
"Where are we going?"
I yelled to the conductor.
"Back to where you came from,"
he answered and I began to cry.

I don't know why the tears
flowed only in my dreams–
I had held them back for so long
while we were stationed in Guam
that part of me withered
and not until returning to the States
was I able to cry again.

Whenever I see the photograph
of the marines hoisting our flag
on Iwo Jima I think of the corpsman,
the roar of the engines,
the precious cargo.

This is what I remember–
yes, put it in your newspaper.
Tell our story.

THE HOUSES THAT HE ENTERED

The man who swore by Apollo
and all the other gods
and goddesses that bear witness
has at last laid down his staff.

Often in his dreams a serpent,
once cleaved by a sword,
slides across a flowered adytum
to rest a leaf upon his brow.

On awakening he sees
the paleness of his hands
instead of Glaucus stolen
from the darkest kingdom.

He closes the doors
to the temple of Asclepios,
drawing strength not from its splendor
but from all the houses that he entered.

THE AILING POEM

The poem was overwhelmed
by all my trusted therapies,
weighted down with attention
and unnecessary medication,
never allowed to free itself
of its restraints, to rise
on its own from the sickbed,
perhaps to even levitate.

And in the end,
or was it the beginning,
I could not bring myself
to bury the ailing poem.
I salvaged a phrase or two,
set flame to what remained
and fanned the fire
with all my breath.